The Spirit of Financial Wellness

> Somewhere between the
> predictable and unpredictable
> absolute and nonsensical
> mean-spirited numbers
> I find humor and solace in
> the Human Psyche.
> — Bonnie Yam

Copyright © 2017 by Bonnie Yam
All rights reserved. This book or any portion thereof may
not be reproduced or used in any manner whatsoever
without the express written permission of the publisher
except for the use of brief quotations in a
book review or scholarly journal.
First Printing: December, 2017
ISBN-13: 978-1979957960
ISBN-10: 1979957967

Pension Maxima Investment Advisory
www.PensionMaxima.com

Financial Wellness Tower
www.FinancialWellnessTower.com

9 Leone Close
Scarsdale, NY 10583
Phone: 914-574-5023

Introduction

Have you noticed an overwhelming abundance of negativity in how we teach Financial Wellness in our country? Look around. You'll often hear:

- "You're spending too much"
- "Don't buy that Starbucks latte"
- "Stick to your budget"

Most of us are fed a constant stream of negativity, while success is triggered by positive emotions and a "can do" attitude.

Start by asking yourself this: How does a child learn?
A child learns the alphabet through song and dance. They get excited about science because of the experiments. What's the common theme behind this?

It's all about having FUN! Learning becomes second nature when you're having fun.

That's why we created Bonnie's Bulls, our Financial Wellness jokebook. We want positive emotions to facilitate new learning.

So, onwards we go!

Start the **learning**, and the **wealth** will **follow**!

About the Author

Bonnie Yam is a Chartered Financial Analyst and an Enrolled Agent with 9 financial titles to her name. She graduated from Smith College with a BA in Mathematics and Economics. She received an MBA in Finance from University of Chicago. Before starting her Qualified Plan business sixteen years ago, she was a Financial Manager for Time Magazine, New York, and a Hedge Fund Research Analyst for Cheetah Investments, Hong Kong. Bonnie has extensive experience in investment management, investment fiduciary and investment education. She is a member of ASPPA, NATP, CFA Institute and NYSSA. When she isn't thinking about numbers, she likes to play piano and writes jokes about the people around her.

Acknowledgements

This book is created with love and care. Special thanks to my cartoonist, Raoul, and my family for their unconditional support throughout this journey.

I also want to thank my loyal supporters who have subscribed to Bonnie's Bulls in the past. Thank you for believing in me, sticking by me and listening to my jokes even when there was ABSOLUTELY nothing crazy funny about them!

Happy

Two friends are sitting happily together.

Bubba: Why are you happy?

Max: I just visited my financial planner. Now I know I won't outlive my money.

Bubba: Me too! I just got diagnosed with heart disease so I won't have too long to live, but my wife is even happier.

Max: Why?

Bubba: Now she knows she can claim on my life insurance policy.

Compulsive Shopping

Maxi: More handbags! You got to be kidding!!! Why are you buying five?!

Penny: I am very sad today. I bought 5 for 5 unhappy incidences that happened to me today. Wife: I missed my alarm, missed my train, bumped into my boss when I entered the office, dropped the coffee on his new shirt.

Maxi: That is only 4 — what about the 5th?

Penny: I got fired!!

Max: I think you'll be needing another handbag then.

Penny: Why?

Max: Because we're getting a divorce!

Magic of Compounding

Max: I am depositing $50 every day into my investment account. That is my daily minimum. I hardly missed a day. I work, work, work and save, save, save. Now I am depositing $500, sometimes even $5,000 a day; and that is how I become a millionaire before 30.

Penny: Hmm…I am doing something similar. My goal is to get everyone to spend at least $50 on our products, my daily minimum. I hit them with incentives, freebies, free trips so they can spend, spend, spend, $50, $500, maybe even $5,000 a day. If I get them to do that, I'll be a billionaire in no time.

Leverage

Max: Tell me about your new trick.
How do you turn one dollar into two?

Junior: You use one dollar as collateral to borrow another dollar from the bank.
Now you have two.

Max: OK. How do you turn two dollars into three?

Junior: Easy. You show the bank how you can earn an extra dollar from the two dollars that you have and they will give you another dollar to play.

Max: OK. How do you turn three dollars into four?

Junior: *Ha!*...you need to learn from the emerging countries in the last financial disaster. You tell the banks that you are going into default. If that happens, no one will get anything, so it's better for them to lend you more so you can buy time to pay them back.

Max: Very good! You learned well, son!

Debt

Polly: *Squawk! Squawk!* I owe you nothing! I owe you nothing!

Mr. Banks: No, no, no… it should be "I-O-U money."

Polly: Nothing! Nothing! It is "I-O-U nothing!"

Mr. Banks: "I-O-U money!" but you owe nothing.

Polly: I-O-U nothing! But you owe nothing!

Mr. Banks: Not true! You owe nothing!

Polly: You owe nothing!

Mr. Banks: Very good. Now say, "I owe something!"

Polly: I owe something!

Mr. Banks: Good!

Polly: *Squawk! Squawk!* Not good!!!

Debt Reduction Country

Supreme Dude: We have recently instituted a new scheme to help our citizens monitor debt.

El Presidente: How?

Supreme Dude: Everyone has to wear a hat! **Green hats** for those who have low debt, a **yellow hat** for those who have unhealthy debt and a **red hat** when their debt gets out of control—but we have to stop very fast.

El Presidente: Why? Do you think the citizens will revolt?

Supreme Dude: No. We will run out of red ink really fast.

Returning Soldiers

Max returns from his tour of duty in Iraq and calls Penny before returning home.

Penny: It's been so long ... I wonder if I will still recognize you. Before I go to the airport, should I get our wedding picture to make sure it is you?

Max: No need, honey. I am basically the same. I have lost some hair and a leg, but the artificial replacement is even sturdier than my old limb. How about you? Are you the same?

Penny: Not the same --- better!

Max arrives and screams.

Max: What happened?!?! How many pounds did you gain?!?! You should have said **heavier** --- not **better!!!**

Two plus Two Equals Two

Penny: What is two plus two?   **Junior:** Two.

Penny: Wrong!

Max: You're actually correct, son! That's how I feel. Doesn't matter how much more I make, the government takes, your mom takes...at the end of the day, two plus two is always two!

Used Car

Max: Can you help me fix my car? I want to sell it.

Mike: How much do you want for it?

Max: $10,000

Mike: That's impossible! This car is old. You have problems with the wheels, the steering, and your mileage is over 100,000.

Max: Just fix everything and don't worry about the mileage. I ordered a new odometer online, so we can just reset it back to zero.

Car Insurance

Max: I can't afford a lot so just give me the State minimum.

Insurance Joe: OK, $200. You get $10,000 for individual, $30,000 for total accident and another $10,000 for property. Pay over there.

Suddenly, a large angry customer walks in. He screams and waves his fists around.

All the employees crawl under the table.

Insurance Joe: Sir, please—please don't hit me! **We don't cover extra body damage insurance**. If you get hurt, you would have to pay hospital fees out of your own pocket. And please remember we also **underinsured your liability insurance**. If you hit anything, you will have to pay. We only cover 50%.

Car Lease

Max: I want to lease the new VESLA SPEEDSTER.

Ms. Daytona: Wow! That is a $100,000 car. Monthly cost is $2,363 a month. Please fill out this application and I will have it ready by tomorrow!

Max comes back the next day:

Max: I thought I applied for a new VESLA SPEEDSTER? Why am I getting a 5 year old VONDA?

Ms. Daytona: Sorry Sir. We checked your credit score and your income and they are both kind of low. Instead of rejecting your application, our boss took pity on you and found you the cheapest lease we have here.

The contract only allows 50% of our standard mileage which is 5,000 FREE miles a year. Please don't drive too much. Anything over $5,000, you will be assessed $.30 for each extra mile. Goodbye and good luck!

Credit Line

Many people line up to make vacation reservations with a premier vacation company. Seeing that there are so many people, the sales agent makes an announcement.

Debbie: Please form two lines. Those who choose to pay with cash, please go to the right. Those who are paying with credit, please go to the left.

After registering, some of the people from the cash line are upset.

Max: Why are those who are paying with credit getting additional spending dollars, free limousine service and a nice vacation bag, while we **Cash Paying Customers** get no incentives?

The agent approaches the microphone to make another announcement.

Debbie: Please note **Credit Buyers**, our interest rate is 22%, with a $30 set-up fee. If you ever miss a payment, your interest rate will be bumped up to 50%. Late fees will include a surcharge of 15%. We'll also need your current house as collateral.
We're so excited to help you open a card with us!

 Getting Married Again

Peggy: Are you getting married again? You just got divorced!

Goldie: I know. But I want to marry again!

Peggy: Are you sure? You'll be investing 10 more years of your life with someone you hardly know and you're only entitled to only 50% of his Social Security benefits.

Goldie (winking)**:** Don't worry—even though I like my new husband even less than my last husband, he's so old and he won't be around very long. I may only get 50% of his benefits now, but I'll be getting 100% when he's dead.

The worst type of loan

Some friends are sitting together crying about having no money.

Bess: I have so much credit card debt. I need to constantly apply for new cards to cover up old loans. I am never going to get out of this rut!

Wendy: I can't even make ends meet till tomorrow. Interest on a two-week payday loan is 400%. I will always be broke!

Kim: I need to lend money to my mother-in-law. It's like kissing money goodbye forever.

Peggy: I lend it to myself and that's worse! The terms, interest and principal change all the time. And, of course, I won't return that money either.

Optometrist

Max: Doctor, I am myopic, unable to focus, and can't read the writing on the wall

Doctor Astigmata: Let's try something.

Doctor Astigmata:
I'll give a prize for reading correctly.
First line: **$100**
Second line: **$500**
Third line: **$1000**
Fourth line: **$1,000,000**

Now, can you read anything?

Max: Actually, I think I can read everything!

Returns

It's the day after Christmas and there is a long line at the **Return Department**. Everyone is returning stuff that they received over Christmas.

Max pulls up a box and gives it to the saleslady.

Saleslady: What is this?

Max: My GPS!

Saleslady: Isn't this the latest model? What's not working?

Max: I type in the place I want to go, but it says,"**Sorry, can't find destination!**"

Saleslady: What did you type?

Max: "Retirement at 40!"

Travel

After hosting a week long competition to encourage people to reduce carbon gas emissions, the company president gets up on stage to announce the winners. The employees start cheering for the creative suggestions of their different departments.

Division VP: Carpooling!   **Millennial:** Biking!

Director: Walking to work!   **Managing Director:** Electric Cars!

The president takes out a card and announces that good ol' Max is the grand prize winner.

Everyone is stunned.

Max, very tired with very dark circles under his eyes walks up to the stage.

Audience: Why is he the winner? What did he do?

President: Max worked in the office for 5 days straight. He even slept in his chair. He never left!!!

Good Food

Some friends are eating at a restaurant and there is a debate on the best way to get great food without paying.

Julius: Pop in at your friend's place around dinner time.

Jackie: Go visit your mom.

Bubba: "Taste test" food at Vostco.

Max calls the waiter to come to the table. The waiter apologizes profusely, immediately takes the food away and promises to remove the item from the bill. Everyone else is surprised.

Irving, Jackie and Bubba: What did you say to the waiter?!?!

Max: I just said I saw a dead fly in the food and I accidentally swallowed it.

Weight Loss Restaurant

Bubba: I hear that people who come to your restaurant do not gain weight. What is your secret?

Tess the Waitress: (Embarrassed) Hmmm…our cook is a little absent minded. He keeps forgetting to add sugar, or leaves out the sauce or dressing. Sometimes, we can't even find the right serving plate, so we serve the same dish in half the size. That's part of the reason…

Bubba: What is the real reason then?

Tess the Waitress: Most of our clients get up and leave without touching the food because they are so upset!

Car Shopping

Bubba: I thought you were getting an AUZI? Isn't that your dream car?

Max: Not anymore. I checked all the resale resources, online, agents, private resellers... everything is out of my reach.

Bubba: So are you going to keep borrowing your dad's car?

Max: I have a better solution. Come, drive with me.

Max takes out a pair of virtual reality glasses and offers one to Bubba.

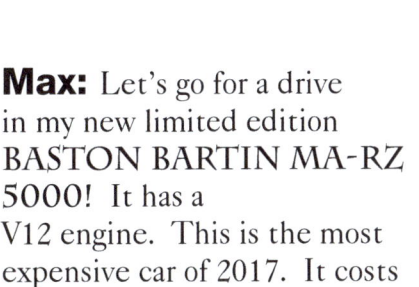

Max: Let's go for a drive in my new limited edition BASTON BARTIN MA-RZ 5000! It has a V12 engine. This is the most expensive car of 2017. It costs only $3,900,000!!!

Inheritance

Dad and son are both watching TV.

Junior: Did you put money in your 401(k)?

Max: Uh huh.

Junior: Did you check your credit card balance?

Max: Yup.

Junior: Do you have a budget?

Max: (Annoyed) Yes, son, but why are you concerned about these things?

Junior: I am just checking on my inheritance.

Hurricane Bruno

Category 3 Hurricane Bruno lands in Tampa Pampa causing massive flooding and damage.

City Accountant: Mayor, we estimate the loss to be over 190 billion. 70% of the houses don't have insurance coverage. We are pretty much screwed.

Mayor of Tampa Pampa: I have a solution! Please call in the reporters for a Press Conference.

Mayor of Tampa Pampa: Hello! I would like to make an important announcement to the world! Please come visit us in Tampa Pampa! Because of Hurricane Bruno, we are now the world's largest NATURAL water park! We have registered 51.88 inches of rain and we will stay submerged for the entire next month. Easiest transportation here is a water taxi...

American Talent

Top winners of AMERICAN TALENT are being interviewed.

Interviewer: How did you get your beautiful singing voice?

1st winner: It's natural. My mom loves CELINE DION, and so I was named Celine and my sister is Dion.

The reporter turns to the 2nd winner who just walks in with her parrot.

Interviewer: You have a beautiful voice too. How did you get such a beautiful voice?

2nd winner: You mean my parrot? I lip sync!

Refundable Office Bonanza

An OFFICE BONANZA ad reads:
Great Deal!
$1 for Copy paper!

Max: What did you buy at OFFICE BONANZA?

Penny: I bought 3 reams of copy paper.

Max: But why were you charged $24?

Penny: It costs $8 per ream, but we only pay $1 because we get $7 store credit after rebates.

Max: So that's why our bill from OFFICE BONANZA keeps growing and growing!
You never apply for the rebates!!!

Flight Volunteer

Bess the Stewardess: Our flight is full. We are offering $500 to anyone who is willing to give up their seat for a later flight today.

There are no takers.

Captain Gilligan: I'm getting desperate. What should we do?

Bess modifies the offer, and 5 passengers immediately walk up to volunteer their seats.

Captain Gilligan: I'm impressed. What did you do?

Bess the Stewardess: I told them they would get the $500 plus I would put them on a flight that's guaranteed to be full.

Captain Gilligan: You mean they can keep earning $500 if they give up their seats again? Smart!

 Ice cream Cake

Bubba wants to propose to his girlfriend and tells the cook to hide the ring inside the cake. They finish the cake, but the ring is nowhere to be found.

Bubba sneaks off and talks to the cook.

Bubba: Where is the ring? Didn't you hide it inside the cake?

Max: Yeah, it's definitely there.

Kim: Owwww!! My stomach hurts!!!

www.ingramcontent.com/pod-product-compliance
Lightning Source LLC
Chambersburg PA
CBHW051935210526
45473CB00006B/2259